MW01064079

SNEAKERHEADS

NEW BALANCE

KENNY ABDO

Fly!
An Imprint of Abdo Zoom
abdobooks.com

abdobooks.com

Published by Abdo Zoom, a division of ABDO, P.O. Box 398166, Minneapolis, Minnesota 55439. Copyright © 2025 by Abdo Consulting Group, Inc. International copyrights reserved in all countries. No part of this book may be reproduced in any form without written permission from the publisher. Fly!™ is a trademark and logo of Abdo Zoom.

Printed in the United States of America, North Mankato, Minnesota.
102024
012025

Photo Credits: Alamy, AP Images, Flickr, Getty Images, Shutterstock,
©Andy Pang p26, 27 / CC BY-NC-ND 4.0
Production Contributors: Kenny Abdo, Jennie Forsberg, Grace Hansen
Design Contributors: Candice Keimig, Neil Klinepier, Laura Graphenteen

Library of Congress Control Number: 2024936559

Publisher's Cataloging-in-Publication Data

Names: Abdo, Kenny, author.
Title: New Balance / by Kenny Abdo
Description: Minneapolis, Minnesota : Abdo Zoom, 2025 | Series: Sneakerheads |
    Includes online resources and index.
Identifiers: ISBN 9781098287467 (lib. bdg.) | ISBN 9781098288167 (ebook) |
    ISBN 9781098288518 (Read-to-me ebook)
Subjects: LCSH: Sneakers--Juvenile literature. | Shoes--Juvenile literature. |
    Fashion--Social aspects--Juvenile literature. | New Balance Athletic Shoe, Inc.
    -Juvenile literature.
Classification: DDC 391.413--dc23

TABLE OF CONTENTS

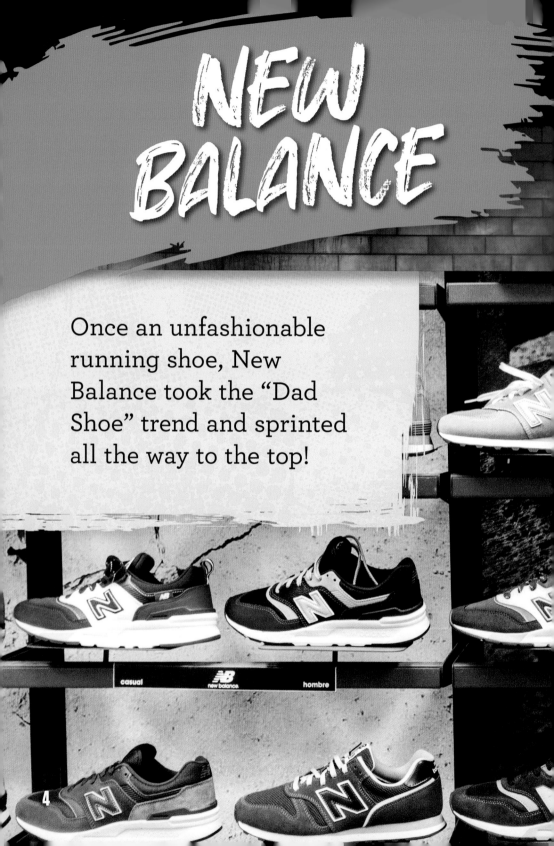

NEW BALANCE

Once an unfashionable running shoe, New Balance took the "Dad Shoe" trend and sprinted all the way to the top!

The **iconic** *N* logo can be spotted on all types of feet from star athletes, to hip-hop legends, and even US presidents!

THE OGs

In 1906, William J. Riley got an idea. While watching some chickens, he noticed their feet were **three-pronged**. This trait keeps the chickens perfectly balanced. Riley wanted to make that possible for humans too.

Riley designed a shoe with three support points. He opened the New Balance **Arch** Support Company in Boston that same year.

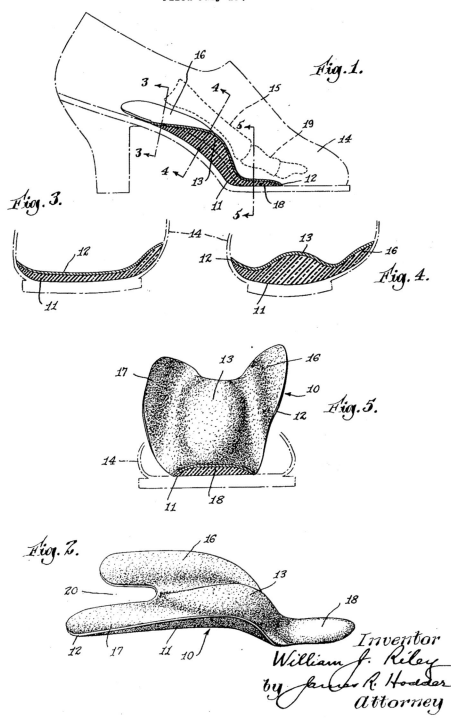

Fig.1.

Fig.3.

Fig.4.

Fig.5.

Fig.7.

Inventor
William J. Riley
by James R. Hodder
Attorney

THE KICKS

New Balance grew by designing footwear for athletes. From cycling to soccer, the shoes helped athletes keep their stability. But the athletes that experienced the most benefits from the shoes were runners.

13

In 1960, New Balance released the Trackster. It was the first running shoe with a rippled sole for traction. This made the Trackster the shoe athlete's ran to in the 1960s!

New Balance created its first shoe with the now-**iconic** *N* logo in 1976. After the **debut** of the 320, *Runner's World* magazine named it the top running shoe.

The world's finest made sneaker.

990

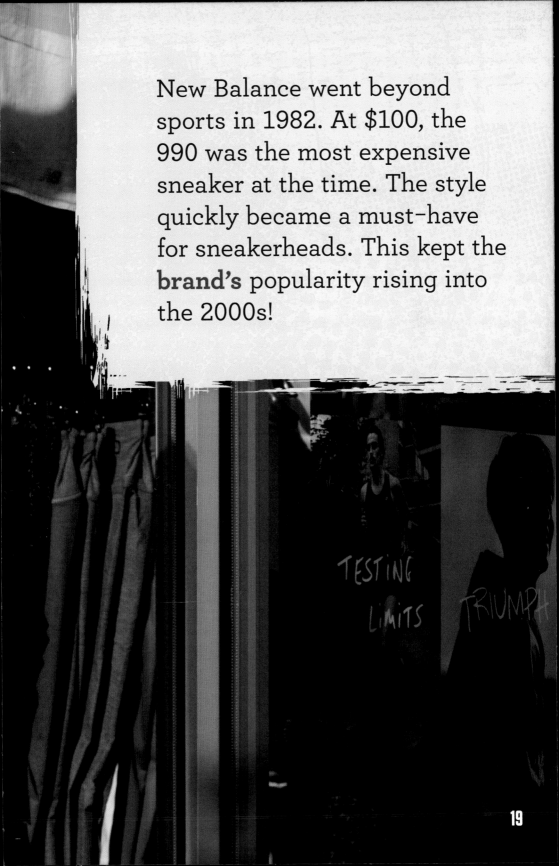

New Balance went beyond sports in 1982. At $100, the 990 was the most expensive sneaker at the time. The style quickly became a must-have for sneakerheads. This kept the **brand's** popularity rising into the 2000s!

New Balance also became a major staple in pop culture. The shoes have been spotted on important figures. Apple founder Steve Jobs, Harry Styles, and music icon Taylor Swift rocked the kicks!

In 2018, New Balance traded in athletics and street **cred** for military service. The **brand** rolled out their 950v2, designed specifically for the US Army. Based on NB's ultra marathon shoe, the 950v2 allowed recruits to train in comfort and style!

New Balance has had an incredible run of **collabs**. The **brand** worked with famous fashion icons such as KITH, Carhartt, and Action Bronson! Together, the companies captured the attention of sneaker enthusiasts around the world.

THE RESTOCK

In 2020, some New Balance shoes became hidden treasure! Fashion designer Salehe Bembury created an **exclusive** pair. Bembury made just 50 pairs and hid them around Los Angeles for fans to find.

Inspired by chicken feet,
New Balance has moved
up to the top of the
sneakerhead pecking order!

GLOSSARY

arch – the curved structure that spans the sole of the foot.

brand – a name, design, or symbol that separates one product from another.

collaboration – a cooperative effort by which people or organizations work together to accomplish a common project or mission.

cred – short for credibility. In pop culture, having popularity with the public, especially young people.

debut – a first appearance.

exclusive – the limited release of merchandise, often with a small number available.

iconic – widely known or easily recognized.

three-pronged – separated into three parts or pieces.

ONLINE RESOURCES

Booklinks
NONFICTION NETWORK
FREE! ONLINE NONFICTION RESOURCES

To learn more about
New Balance, please visit
abdobooklinks.com or scan
this QR code. These links
are routinely monitored
and updated to provide the
most current information
available.

INDEX